BACH
for the 'CELLO

TEN PIECES IN THE FIRST POSITION

Transcribed for Violoncello and Piano by
CHARLES KRANE

Ed. 2010

G. SCHIRMER, Inc.

DISTRIBUTED BY

HAL•LEONARD®
CORPORATION
7777 W. BLUEMOUND RD. P.O. BOX 13819 MILWAUKEE, WI 53213

CONTENTS

NOTE

The purpose of these transcriptions in the first position is to enable the young violoncello pupil to play and enjoy Bach after one year or less of instruction.

Bach's Suites for Solo Violoncello and Sonatas for Violoncello and Piano are so difficult technically that years of practice are required before a student can attempt to play them.

It is hoped that these pieces will prove to be a useful addition to the limited repertoire of the beginning Violoncellist.

EXPLANATION OF SIGNS, ABBREVIATIONS, TEMPO MARKS, AND DYNAMICS

$\bar{\rho}$ . . . . A line above a note indicates that it is to be played broadly.

$\frown$ . . . . A Hold (a prolonged note or rest).

⌒ . . . . { A Slur. Different notes under a curved line are to be played in the same stroke.

⌒ . . . . { A Tie. When the curved line connects two notes of the same pitch, the second note is a continuation of the first one and is played without a stop between the notes.

. . . . . . { This type of bowing indicates that the notes are to be detached and separated from one another, whether they are tied or slurred. This is done by stopping the bow after the first note and continuing the stroke in the same direction for the second note, without removing the bow from the string.

W. B. . . . . Whole Bow

L. H. . . . . Lower-half of the Bow

L. Q. . . . . Lower-quarter of the Bow

M. . . . . Middle of the Bow

U. H. . . . . Upper-half of the Bow

U. Q. . . . . Upper-quarter of the Bow

Fr. . . . . Frog (or Nut)

Allegro . . . . Quick, lively

Andante . . . . Moderate. The word *Andante* literally means "going"

Con moto . . . . With motion, rather quick

Grazioso . . . . In a graceful style

Maestoso . . . . With dignity or majesty

Moderato . . . . Moderately

In modo di Marcia . . . . In March time

f (*forte*) . . . . Loud

mf (*mezzo forte*) . . . . Medium loud

p (*piano*) . . . . Soft

mp (*mezzo piano*) . . . . Medium soft

pp (*pianissimo*) . . . . Very soft

cresc. { . . . . Crescendo (gradually louder)

dim. { . . . . Diminuendo (gradually softer)

poco ritard. . . . . Gradually slower

(♩ = 88) . . . . This indicates that when the metronome is set at 88 each half-note has the duration of one beat of the metronome.

Bach for the 'Cello

Johann Sebastian Bach
Transcribed by Charles Krane

March in G

Sarabande

Arioso

Minuet in C

Bach for the 'Cello

March in G

Johann Sebastian Bach
Transcribed by Charles Krane

Violoncello

Sarabande

Arioso

Minuet in C

poco ritard.

Air

Minuet in E minor

Andante

Gigue

Chorale

March in D

Air

Minuet in E minor

Andante

Gigue

Chorale

March in D